Cornerstones of Freedom

Williamsburg

Zachary Kent

CHILDRENS PRESS®

CHICAGO

Library of Congress Cataloging-in-Publication Data

Kent, Zachary.
Williamsburg / by Zachary Kent.

  p. cm. — (Cornerstones of freedom)
 Summary: A history of Virginia's colonial capital from
its earliest days through its restoration into a major
tourist attraction.
 ISBN 0-516-04854-6
 1. Williamsburg (Va.)—History—Juvenile literature.
[1. Williamsburg (Va.)—History.] I. Title. II. Series.
F234.W7K46 1992
975.5'4252—dc20

91-35055
CIP
AC

The sleepy town of Williamsburg, Virginia, buzzed with excitement on June 12, 1928. In the evening darkness, men and women hurried along the sidewalks past charming houses, shops, and stores that dated back to the 1700s. Many other old buildings, shacks, and sheds stood crumbling among modern movie theaters, poolrooms, and gas stations. Once the colonial capital of Virginia, Williamsburg had changed a great deal over the years, its glory days forgotten by nearly everyone.

Inside the high-school auditorium, hundreds of townspeople jammed into seats and stood

Williamsburg's historic Duke of Gloucester Street

Dr. William Goodwin

along walls. The room hummed with gossip as everyone waited for the town meeting to begin. Some stared curiously at the Reverend Dr. William Goodwin, former rector of Bruton Parish Church. Most of the people knew that Dr. Goodwin was fascinated with the history of Williamsburg. He talked constantly of wanting to repair the town's colonial buildings and monuments. In December 1926, Dr. Goodwin had suddenly begun buying Williamsburg real estate. Whenever an old house or empty lot was for sale, the reverend snapped it up. People scratched their heads and wondered where Dr. Goodwin was getting so much money. Rumors quickly spread that a millionaire had asked him to try to buy the entire town.

At 8:00 P.M., the noise in the auditorium died down as the gray-haired minister walked across the stage. To a hushed audience, Goodwin admitted that he and his "associates" wished to buy the Williamsburg town greens and other public properties so that eventually the whole town could be restored as a "national shrine." "The donors of the money to restore Williamsburg," Dr. Goodwin revealed to his listeners, "are Mr. and Mrs. John D. Rockefeller, Jr., of New York."

The auditorium burst into loud applause. Excitedly, the townspeople voted to help with restoration plans. John D. Rockefeller, Jr., was

Jamestown was Virginia's first English settlement.

one of the richest men in the world. No one
doubted that he could make Dr. Goodwin's dream
come true. In the most ambitious program of
restoration and reconstruction ever attempted,
the colonial capital of Williamsburg, Virginia,
would live again.

Virginia's colonial history began in 1607, when
English adventurers established a settlement on
swampy land along the James River. The village,
which they named Jamestown, served as the
colony's first capital. The settlers cleared the land
and planted tobacco crops in the rich soil. In
1633, on higher ground several miles away, hardy
pioneers chopped down trees and built an

outpost to defend against Indian attacks. The outpost and its scattered cabins came to be known as Middle Plantation.

For years, mosquitoes rose in clouds from the swamps around Jamestown, spreading disease and death. Many Virginians complained that Jamestown was a poor place for their capital. In 1699, fire swept through the town. The statehouse collapsed to the ground in charred ruins. Legislators decided it was time to relocate the colonial capital to nearby Middle Plantation.

A few handsome brick buildings already stood at Middle Plantation. The College of William and Mary, the second-oldest institution of higher

An early engraving of the College of William and Mary

Duke of Gloucester Street as it looked in the early 1700s

learning in the American colonies, had been
established there by royal charter in 1693.
Virginia's royal governor, Francis Nicholson,
drew up plans to make the new capital the finest
city in all the American colonies. It would be
named Williamsburg in honor of England's King
William III.

Across 220 acres of sprawling woods and
fields, Nicholson put teams to work with axes
and shovels. Sweating laborers cleared a wide
main avenue. Named Duke of Gloucester Street
in honor of the son of Queen Anne, it stretched
from the college nearly a mile to the site of the
new capitol building. Two other long streets,

Francis Nicholson

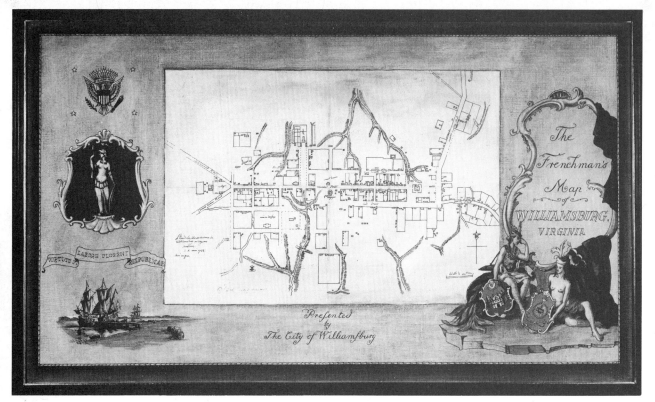

A plan of Williamsburg from the 1700s

Alexander Spotswood

Francis and Nicholson, were laid out parallel to this central roadway. On one-half-acre plots, bricklayers and carpenters gradually built townhouses, shops, and taverns.

The royal governors who followed after Nicholson continued the construction of Williamsburg's official buildings. Virginia's colonial lawmakers first met in the handsome brick Capitol in 1704. Lieutenant Governor Alexander Spotswood supervised the completion of the city's octagonal Powder Magazine in 1715 and watched laborers finish work on the sturdy brick Public Gaol (jail). Strolling through carefully landscaped flower gardens, Spotswood

An aerial view of the Governor's Palace and gardens

smiled proudly as workers at last completed the
elegant Governor's Palace in 1722.

"They dwell comfortably . . . pleasantly, and
plentifully in this delightful, healthful, and
(I hope) thriving city of Williamsburg," wrote the
Reverend Hugh Jones of his fellow townspeople.
By the middle of the 1700s, some two thousand
Virginians—half free whites and half black
slaves—lived in Williamsburg. Twice a week,
neighboring farmers steered wagons brimming
with vegetables, fruits, and other produce into
the city. With baskets on their arms, citizens and

servants walked among the wooden stalls at Market Square haggling over prices and buying fresh foods.

Along Williamsburg's tree-lined streets, general stores and crafts shops conducted daily business. Hammers clanked on iron horseshoes beside hot blacksmith forges. Gunsmiths fashioned handmade rifles and pistols. Jewelers tinkered with watches and clocks. The rasping sound of saws and files could be heard at carpenters' and cabinetmakers' shops, while the smell of oiled leather drifted from the shops of saddle makers and shoemakers. Tailors and seamstresses sewed

Wheelwrights (left) and spinners (below) were among the craftspeople who lived and worked in bustling colonial Williamsburg.

From 1699 to 1780, Williamsburg was the center of Virginia government and politics. Here, men in colonial dress reenact the procedure of voting at the courthouse.

clothes with needle and thread. Milliners stocked shelves with ladies' hats, fans, and gloves. Wig makers combed and powdered wigs for gentlemen customers.

Williamsburg especially came alive twice a year, in the spring and fall, when people came from all over Virginia to attend meetings of the General Court, the colony's highest court. During these "Publick Times," planters, lawyers, and elected representatives arrived on horseback and in painted carriages. Wealthy men brought their families and stayed in townhouses they owned.

A conference room in the reconstructed Capitol

Most men, however, found beds and meals at taverns, where they drank, gambled, and told stories late into the night. Josiah Chowning advertised his tavern in 1766 by stating that "all who please to favour me with their custom may depend on the best of entertainment for themselves, servants, and horses, and good pasturage."

Virginia's legislative body, the general assembly, was usually in session during the Publick Times. People jammed along Duke of Gloucester Street to watch the royal governor pass in his fine coach on his way to the Capitol to open each session of the general assembly. In the plain, paneled chamber of the House of

Burgesses, elected burgesses voted on colonial laws for Virginia. Upstairs in another room sat the twelve men of the Governor's Council. These councillors, appointed by the king, gave the royal governor valuable advice.

In the evenings, invited guests rode to the Governor's Palace. Williamsburg was the cultural center of the Virginia Colony, and a dance at the Governor's Palace was always a celebrated event. Chandeliers and punch bowls glittered with light in the ballroom. Ladies dressed in fine satin gowns and gentlemen wearing silk breeches, lacy shirts, and tight-fitting waistcoats smiled as they danced the minuet.

Fancy balls were celebrated events in colonial Williamsburg.

A young George Washington

Williamsburg witnessed many historic scenes through the years. On September 3, 1755, a tall, muscular, twenty-three-year-old man trotted on horseback down Duke of Gloucester Street. Newly appointed Colonel George Washington was riding off to take command of Virginia's militia during the French and Indian War. In 1758, Frederick County citizens elected Colonel Washington to the House of Burgesses. When the government was in session, Washington lived in a house owned by his wife, Martha Custis Washington.

During the early 1760s, another famous Virginian lived in Williamsburg. After graduating from the College of William and Mary, young Thomas Jefferson began studying law in the office of George Wythe. A respected public leader, Wythe owned a handsome brick mansion on Palace Street.

In 1765, Americans throughout the thirteen colonies were grumbling about their rights. Many complained that King George III gave them no voice in the British Parliament. To pay the huge costs of winning the French and Indian War, Parliament had passed the Stamp Act, which taxed documents and paper goods sent to America. In Williamsburg, a young burgess named Patrick Henry introduced into the House of Burgesses several resolutions condemning the Stamp Act. Henry argued fiercely that passage of

As a young man, Thomas Jefferson (top left) studied law in the Williamsburg law office of George Wythe (bottom left). Wythe, a respected public leader, owned a handsome brick mansion on Palace Street (above).

his resolutions would show that the colonists would never stand for English tyranny.

"Treason!" shouted shocked burgesses loyal to the king.

"If this be treason," challenged Henry, "make the most of it!"

Thrilled by his defiant words, a majority of the burgesses passed Henry's "Virginia Resolves," which soon became famous throughout the colonies.

In the face of so much protest, the British Parliament repealed the Stamp Act in 1766. It

The historic Raleigh Tavern

soon passed other equally unfair laws, however. In 1769, Virginians learned of the new British Revenue Act, which taxed certain imported goods. The angry debate that followed in Williamsburg made Royal Governor Norborne Berkeley so worried that he dissolved the House of Burgesses. The abrupt closing of the doors of the Capitol failed to stop the protesting burgesses. In a bold move, they gathered farther down Duke of Gloucester Street, at the Raleigh Tavern. Crowded into the tavern's large Apollo Room, the men voted to defy royal authority and declare a boycott of British import items.

Massachusetts colonists protested a hated tax on tea by dumping cargoes of British tea into

Boston Harbor in December 1773. Virginia burgesses cheered when they heard of this "Boston Tea Party." Soon afterward, the Earl of Dunmore, Virginia's newest royal governor, nervously dissolved the House of Burgesses again. Meeting at the Raleigh Tavern, the burgesses swiftly called for a meeting of representatives from all of the thirteen colonies. In September 1774, Peyton Randolph, George Washington, Patrick Henry, and other Virginia delegates journeyed to Philadelphia to attend the First Continental Congress.

Alarmed by growing talk of rebellion, Governor Dunmore asked British marines to remove gunpowder from the Powder Magazine on Market Square on the night of April 20, 1775. The next morning, a mob of furious colonists led by Patrick Henry crowded outside the Governor's Palace. They demanded either the return of the gunpowder or payment for it. Meekly, Governor Dunmore agreed to pay for the powder.

The Powder Magazine

Virginians soon received word that clashes between Massachusetts minutemen and British redcoats had occurred at Lexington and Concord on April 19. With revolutionary spirit, seventeen-year-old William and Mary student James Monroe (the future fifth U.S. president) joined other men in a raid on the Powder Magazine. With captured guns and powder, these Williamsburg rebels marched off to fight.

Only total freedom from Britain would do now, argued Virginians meeting in a convention at Williamsburg in May 1776. In resolutions sent to Philadelphia, they urged, "These United Colonies are, and of right ought to be, free and independent States." As a result, Thomas Jefferson, a Virginia delegate at the Second Continental Congress, penned the Declaration of Independence. On July 4, 1776, Jefferson and the six other Virginia delegates at Philadelphia's Independence Hall joined the delegates of the other twelve colonies in signing the document. Thus a new nation, the "United States of America," was born.

Already, Virginia's patriot leaders in Williamsburg had created the Commonwealth of Virginia. Delegate George Mason had drafted a bill of rights and had helped write a Virginia constitution. At the Governor's Palace, Patrick Henry served as the state's first governor until Thomas Jefferson was elected in 1779. That year, a great change occurred at Williamsburg. Virginia's government, worrying that Williamsburg's location made it too easy for the British to attack, voted to move the capital to Richmond.

Drums rattled in the streets of Williamsburg during the last days of September 1781. Dust choked the air as General George Washington's Continental army marched toward the nearby town of Yorktown. A few weeks later, wild cheers

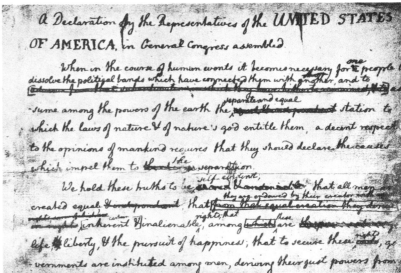

Left: Thomas Jefferson writing the Declaration of Independence
Right: Part of a rough draft of the famous document

and celebrations greeted the soldiers as they marched back. American triumph over Lord Cornwallis' British army at Yorktown meant the United States finally had won its war for independence.

With the end of the fighting, quiet and calm settled over Williamsburg. Fire burned the Governor's Palace to the ground in December 1781, but there seemed no reason to rebuild it. In time, the colonial spirit of Williamsburg faded from memory. During the American Civil War, between 1861 and 1865, Confederate and Union soldiers tramped back and forth through the streets. Over the years, the town sank into a

By the 1920s, many of Williamsburg's colonial-era buildings had been torn down, while many others had fallen into ruin (above).

condition of general ruin. Weeds and ivy strangled untended gardens. Fences fell down and roofs sagged. Some neglected buildings and homes rotted, while others were destroyed by fire. By the 1920s, the Powder Magazine was being used as a garage. A general store stood where the Raleigh Tavern had been. The town's high school rose on the foundations of the Governor's Palace. Banks, supermarkets, and other buildings cluttered half of Market Square, and telephone poles jutted along the center divider of paved Duke of Gloucester Street.

While such other former colonial capitals as

New York City, Boston, and Philadelphia boomed with spectacular growth, Williamsburg slept, all but forgotten. The town's former glory completely captured the imagination of one man, however. The Reverend Dr. William Goodwin first arrived in Williamsburg in 1902. While serving as rector of Bruton Parish Church, he grew excited about the local history. Raising donations and hiring workers, Goodwin repaired the church so that it looked as lovely as it had when it was built in 1715.

In 1908, Goodwin was called away to minister at a church in Rochester, New York. In 1923, however, the College of William and Mary hired him as a teacher and fundraiser. Upon his return

The Bruton Parish Church was the first colonial structure in Williamsburg to be restored to its former glory through Dr. Goodwin's efforts.

to Williamsburg, Dr. Goodwin was shocked to see how many houses and buildings had decayed while he was gone. The sight of cheap diners, movie theaters, and gas stations standing along the historic streets saddened him. Goodwin dreamed of somehow restoring the entire town to its original colonial beauty. "The ghosts of the past haunted the houses and walked the streets at night," he exclaimed.

Dr. Goodwin decided to find a millionaire to help him keep the noble history of Williamsburg alive. In 1924, he penned a letter to Edsel Ford, son of carmaker Henry Ford. "Seriously, I want your father to buy Williamsburg, the old colonial capital of Virginia," Goodwin wrote. "Other men have bought rare books and preserved historic houses. No man has yet had the vision and courage to buy and preserve a Colonial village."

When the Ford family failed to take an interest in the project, Goodwin next approached John D. Rockefeller, Jr. Rockefeller ran the hugely successful Standard Oil Company founded by his father. Over the years, he had given generous donations to many worthy causes.

Twice in 1926, Rockefeller visited Williamsburg. As Dr. Goodwin excitedly showed him around the town, pointing out historic buildings, Rockefeller's eyes flickered with interest. He agreed quietly to pay for some architectural drawings that would show what the

*John D. Rockefeller, Jr., (right) talks with Dr. Goodwin (left)
during a visit to Williamsburg in 1928.*

restored town would look like. In December
1926, Dr. Goodwin telegraphed a message to
Rockefeller's office in New York City. The old
colonial Ludwell-Paradise House was for sale for
only eight thousand dollars. Rockefeller made a
quick decision and telegraphed back permission
for the purchase. To a friend, the millionaire
confided, "It is my desire and purpose to carry
out this enterprise completely and entirely . . . to
restore Williamsburg . . . to what it was in
colonial days."

In secret partnership with Rockefeller, Dr.
Goodwin began buying every piece of
Williamsburg real estate that came on the

William G. Perry

market. Prices skyrocketed as Williamsburg citizens tried to guess the source of Dr. Goodwin's money. "We're going to buy the town!" Goodwin revealed joyfully to William G. Perry, the chief architect he hired. By the spring of 1928, the minister had spent $2 million buying thirty-seven different Williamsburg properties. At the College of William and Mary, workers hammered together scaffolding and began renovating the handsome, 230-year-old brick Wren Building. On Francis Street, laborers started repairs on the colonial Bracken House.

Townspeople crowded into the high-school auditorium on the evening of June 12, 1928. They gasped with excitement as Dr. Goodwin at last revealed Rockefeller's name and his plans for Williamsburg. With local support, Colonial Williamsburg, Inc. continued buying the rest of the private dwellings in the town. Some citizens refused to sell their old houses because they had nowhere else to go. Dr. Goodwin solved that problem by arranging for them to become "life tenants." In exchange for a yearly rent of one dollar, they could live in their restored houses for the rest of their lives.

During the next few years, Williamsburg hummed with activity. Bulldozers and wrecking balls knocked down some 720 unwanted modern buildings. Brick by brick and board by board, engineers restored 88 original colonial buildings.

The Raleigh Tavern during its reconstruction in the 1920s

They stripped false fronts off some and replaced rotting beams in others. They paid attention to every tiny detail. Planning to reconstruct more than 400 lost houses and stores, architects spread across the Virginia countryside to study existing colonial buildings. They filled notebooks with drawings of such details as window-frame designs, proper fireplace and chimney construction, and roof-shingling methods. Scholarly researchers carefully studied Williamsburg historical records and old photographs. Archaeologists dug up the ground in search of reconstruction clues. Antiques experts purchased authentic tables, chairs, and other 1700s furnishings with which to fill the

The colonial Capitol (left) and Governor's Palace (right) were both rebuilt on their original sites.

houses. Chief landscape architect Arthur A. Shurcliff designed 81 acres of beautiful gardens.

By 1934, the giant task of restoring Williamsburg had progressed far enough for the town to be officially opened to the public. From the steps of the Wren Building, President Franklin D. Roosevelt proclaimed Duke of Gloucester Street "the most historic avenue in America." Soon, hosts and hostesses in colonial dress welcomed tourists to the reconstructed Governor's Palace, Capitol, Raleigh's Tavern, and other buildings. These knowledgeable "townspeople" gladly answered questions about Williamsburg's history.

The dining room at Bassett Hall

Until his death in 1939, Dr. Goodwin enjoyed the thrill of seeing his dream unfold. The sponsor of Colonial Williamsburg, John D. Rockefeller, Jr., also took a continuing interest in the project. Twice a year, Rockefeller vacationed at Williamsburg, staying at Bassett Hall, the colonial mansion he owned at the edge of town. While there, he would walk along the streets, deciding which houses needed fresh paint and pointing out hedges that needed to be clipped. By the time he died in 1960, Rockefeller's backing of the Williamsburg project had cost him over $100 million.

Today, Williamsburg's attractions include the DeWitt Wallace Decorative Arts Gallery and the Abby Aldrich Rockefeller Folk Art Center, both run by the Colonial Williamsburg Foundation. Tourists may also wander through the orchards and gardens of Carter's Grove, a working colonial-style plantation eight miles away. Williamsburg itself, however, remains the greatest attraction of all, drawing in millions of visitors who wish to experience living history.

Every day, the colonial capital bustles with activity as its "townspeople" go about their business. Horsemen in three-cornered hats trot along shady lanes, and women in hoop skirts stoop to smell the tulips in lovely flower gardens.

A Williamsburg garden

Today, visitors to Williamsburg can watch costumed "townspeople" demonstrate the daily activities of colonial life.

Behind houses, servants sweep out kitchens, wash laundry in wooden tubs, and sprinkle feed for chickens. In stores throughout the town, merchants sell soap, candles, and many other colonial items. Dozens of skilled craftspeople ply their trades at their shops. Coopers split wood into strips and bend iron hoops for barrels. At apothecary shops, druggists mix colonial medicines and sell lemon drops and candy sticks.

Virginia's first newspaper, the *Virginia Gazette*, began publication in 1736. At the printing office on Duke of Gloucester Street, workers lay type and mix ink for the latest edition. At mealtimes, taverns such as Christiana Campbell's and the

Kings Arms are as crowded as they ever were in colonial times. Tourists may dine on Virginia ham, crabcakes, roast potatoes, corn muffins, and other delicious colonial foods.

At the Public Gaol, on Nicholson Street, the cells still stand where thirteen of Blackbeard's pirates awaited hanging in the early 1700s. On the grass at Market Square, "militiamen" can sometimes be seen firing their muskets and marching in drill practice.

Perhaps the richest feeling of history comes from a visit to Bruton Parish Church, where George Washington and other Virginia leaders prayed during troubled times. A walk into the reconstructed Capitol brings forth the ghosts of Patrick Henry and his revolutionary comrades.

A cannon-firing demonstration by Williamsburg "militiamen"

Visiting Williamsburg is like taking a step back in time.

"What a temptation to sit in silence and let the past speak to us of those great patriots whose voices once resounded in these halls," John D. Rockefeller, Jr., once said.

The spirit of American independence remains alive in Williamsburg, America's greatest experiment in preserving the past. Thomas Jefferson once called the town "the finest school of manners and morals in America." Thanks to the vision of Dr. William Goodwin and the support of John D. Rockefeller, Jr., visitors who walk Williamsburg's streets today can still learn priceless lessons about our nation's character.

INDEX

PHOTO CREDITS

Picture Identifications:
Cover: A reenactment in Williamsburg's Market Square of drill practice by a colonial fife-and-drum corps
Page 1: The restored Wren Building at the College of William and Mary
Page 2: One of Williamsburg's costumed interpreters

Project Editor: Shari Joffe
Designer: Karen Yops
Cornerstones of Freedom Logo: David Cunningham

ABOUT THE AUTHOR

Zachary Kent grew up in Little Falls, New Jersey, and received a degree in English from St. Lawrence University. After college, he worked at a New York City literary agency for two years and then launched his writing career. To support himself while writing, he has worked as a taxi driver, a shipping clerk, and a house painter.

Mr. Kent has had a lifelong interest in American history. Studying the United States presidents was his childhood hobby. His collection of presidential items includes books, pictures, and games, as well as several autographed letters.